SARDINIA

Travel Guide 2023

Mariana Coxtez

Sardinia Travel Guide 2023

An Updated Comprehensive Guide to Sardinia and Everything you need to know for first Time Visitors

By Mariana Coxtez

Copyright

Table of Contents

Introduction

Deborah and Peter had always dreamed of visiting Sardinia, the picturesque Italian island known for its stunning beaches, clear waters, and rich history. After years of planning and saving, they finally made their way to the island for their much-anticipated vacation.

Their first day in Sardinia was a whirlwind of sights, sounds, and smells. They visited the local markets and sampled the fresh seafood, cured meats, and cheeses that the island is famous for. They strolled along the cobbled streets of the old town, admiring the medieval architecture and colorful buildings. And they basked in the warm Mediterranean sun on the white sand beaches that stretched for miles.

As the days passed, Deborah and Peter became more adventurous. They rented a car and drove deep into the heart of the island, exploring the rugged terrain and winding roads. They hiked through the mountains and valleys, marveling at the ancient ruins and hidden caves.

One day, they stumbled upon a tiny village nestled in the hills. The village was like something out of a storybook, with narrow streets and stone houses huddled together. The locals were warm and friendly, and they invited Deborah and Peter to join them for a traditional feast.

The feast was a revelation. Deborah and Peter tasted dishes they had never imagined, each one more delicious than the last. They sipped local wines and spirits, and danced to the lively music played by the villagers.

As the night wore on, Deborah and Peter realized that they had fallen in love with Sardinia. They had never felt so alive, so connected to a place and its people. They knew that their memories of the island would stay with them forever, and that they would come back again and again to relive this unforgettable experience.

History and Culture of Sardinia

The second-largest island in the area after Sicily is Sardinia, a stunning island in the Mediterranean Sea. Since prehistoric times, the island has had a rich history and culture. The Phoenicians, Carthaginians, Romans, Vandals, Byzantines, Arabs, Genoese, and Spanish were a some of the groups who resided on the island over the years. These many populations that have lived on the island throughout the ages have shaped the island's distinctive and varied culture.

Nuragic Civilization and Prehistory

The Neolithic era marks the beginning of Sardinia's extensive prehistory. There are many historic ruins on the island, including tombs, temples, and other buildings from the Bronze and Iron Ages. The Nuraghe, an old stone structure type exclusive to Sardinia, is one of the most prominent ancient structures on the island. The Nuragic Civilization, which existed from roughly 1800 BC to 238 BC, is thought to have been responsible for the construction of these Nuraghe.

The earliest significant civilisation on the island was the Nuragic civilisation, which was renowned for its highly developed construction abilities and military strength. The huge stone forts that the Nuragic people constructed, known as Nuraghe, served as defensive fortifications. In addition to mastering metallurgy, they created a sophisticated irrigation system. Before being subdued by the Romans, the Nuragic Civilization flourished for more than a thousand years.

Ancient Rome

Sardinia was taken over by the Roman Empire in 238 BC, and the island soon rose to prominence as a major hub for trade and agriculture. In addition to constructing countless roads, aqueducts, and other public works, the Romans also introduced a variety of novel farming practices to the island. Additionally, the Romans brought Christianity to the island, which later developed into a significant religious hub in the area.

the Middle Ages

Several peoples, notably the Vandals, Byzantines, and Arabs, conquered Sardinia during the Middle Ages. The island of Sardinia developed into a cultural melting pot as a result of the influences of these numerous ethnicities. Both innovative architectural designs, like the horseshoe arch, and new agricultural methods, such irrigation systems and the production of citrus fruits, were brought about by the Arabs.

Spain's reign:

Sardinia was incorporated into the Kingdom of Spain in the fourteenth century after being conquered by the Kingdom of Aragon. The island has been affected for a long time by the more than 400 years of Spanish control. The Spanish contributed new architectural designs like the Baroque and Renaissance styles as well as new agricultural practices like the growing of grapes for wine.

Culture and Cuisine:

Sardinia has a distinct and complex culture that has been affected by its long and varied history. The island is well-known for its annual festivities and celebrations. The Carnival of Mamoiada, held in February, is one of the island's most prominent celebrations, celebrating the island's old customs.

Sardinian cuisine is also inspired by the island's history and culture. The cuisine is noted for its basic and rustic flavors, which are based on locally available ingredients. The roast suckling pig is a popular special occasion meal on the island.

Sardinia Population

The island has a population of about 1.6 million inhabitants, making it one of the least inhabited regions in Italy.

Sardinians, Italians, and immigrants from all over the world make up the island's diversified population. Sardinians, an ethnic group with its own language and culture, make up the vast bulk of the population. They account for over 60% of the population, with the remainder made up of Italian and other European immigrants.

Sardinia's population is mostly rural, with most people residing in small towns and villages scattered around the island. Cagliari, the island's major city, with a population of roughly 150,000 people. Other important cities are Sassari, Olbia, and Alghero.

Sardinia's urban centers are comprised of these cities and several smaller villages.

Sardinia's population is largely constant, with a low birth rate and low immigration rate. This has resulted in an aging population, with a median age of roughly 47 years old. The population is likewise highly skewed toward women, with around 52% of the population being female. This is attributable to a multitude of causes, including higher female life expectancy and a higher male emigration rate.

Sardinia has a high level of linguistic diversity, with numerous different languages and dialects spoken on the island. The official language is Italian, but many people also speak Sardinian, a Romance language with roots in Latin. Other languages spoken on the island include Catalan, Spanish, and English, notably in tourist regions.

Sardinia's economy is built mostly on tourism, agriculture, and manufacturing. The tourist business is an important source of income for the island, with millions of people coming to enjoy the island's beaches, historic sites, and natural beauty. Agriculture is also important on the island, with grapes, olives, and wheat being among the crops grown. Manufacturing is concentrated in metropolitan areas, including businesses such as food processing, textiles, and electronics.

Finally, Sardinia is a distinct and diverse territory with a limited population. The island's population is made up of a diverse mix of ethnic groups and cultures, with a high level of linguistic variety. Despite its small size, the island has a rich history and a robust economy, with tourism, agriculture, and industry being the key industries.

Sardinia Religion

Sardinia has been home to a variety of religions and religious activities throughout its history, including both indigenous and imported traditions.

The Nuragic religion, which populated the island from the Bronze Age until the 2nd century BC, was the earliest known religion practiced on Sardinia. The worship of female deities was central to Nuragic religion, with the Mother Goddess being the most important figure. The Nuragic people, like the Egyptians, believed in an afterlife and conducted ritual sacrifice.

Sardinia was invaded and occupied by a variety of peoples over the centuries that followed, including the Phoenicians, Carthaginians, Romans, and Vandals. Each of these communities carried their own religious traditions with them, and many of these traditions merged with the pre-existing Nuragic religion to form the island's unique religious environment.

Saint Efisio, a Christian martyr who is still revered on the island today, was one of the most important religious figures in Sardinia throughout the Middle Ages. Saint Efisio is credited with saving Sardinian citizens from a plague in the 17th century, and his feast day, May 1st, is a prominent event in Sardinian religious and cultural life.

The Madonna degli Angeli, a Marian apparition who is supposed to have appeared to a shepherd in the 16th century, is another major figure in Sardinian religion. The Madonna degli Angeli is considered as the island's protector, and her picture can be found in churches and chapels all around Sardinia.

Sardinia is now primarily Catholic, with the Catholic Church playing a significant role in the island's religious and cultural life. However, the island also has a number of other religious traditions, such as Protestantism, Judaism, and Islam.

There has been growing interest in Sardinia's pre-Christian religious traditions in recent years, with many Sardinians attempting to reclaim and resuscitate these old practices. As a result, a new movement known as Sardinian neo-paganism has emerged, attempting to mix elements of the island's traditional traditions with modern spiritual practices.

Overall, the religious landscape of Sardinia is rich and multidimensional, reflecting the island's long and diverse past. Religion continues to play an essential role in the life of this unique and intriguing island, whether through the worship of ancient deities or the devotion of Christian saints.

Dos and Don't in Sardinia

For first-time visitors to Sardinia, there are some dos and don'ts to bear in mind to ensure a nice and hassle-free experience. In this article, we will present a complete guide to help you traverse the island like a local.

Dos:

Try the local cuisine: Sardinian cuisine is noted for its unique flavors and ingredients. Some of the most popular dishes are "porceddu" (roasted suckling pig), "culurgiones" (Sardinian ravioli), and "pann'e saba" (Sardinian honey bread). During your visit, try some of the island's traditional cuisine.

Do visit the beaches: Sardinia is recognized for its immaculate beaches, crystal-clear waves, and lovely bays. Cala Mariolu, Spiaggia del Principe, and Cala

Luna are some of the most stunning beaches. Pack sunscreen, a hat, and a beach blanket for a pleasant day by the water.

Do visit historical places: Sardinia has a rich cultural heritage, with historical sites dating back to prehistoric times. The Nuraghe Su Nuraxi, a UNESCO World Heritage Site, and Cagliari's Roman Amphitheater are two must-see sites. These attractions provide an opportunity to learn about the island's fascinating history and culture.

While public transportation is accessible, hiring a car is the best way to explore the island. It lets you to explore at your own leisure and find hidden jewels that would otherwise be inaccessible by bus or train.

Learn some fundamental Italian phrases: Although many people on the island speak English, knowing some basic Italian phrases will help you converse with locals and make your experience more pleasurable. Some essential phrases to learn include "ciao" (hello/goodbye), "per favore" (please), and "grazie" (thank you).

Don'ts:

Don't leave valuables unattended: As with any tourist site, it's crucial to keep a watch on your possessions. Avoid leaving valuables unattended on the beach or in your car, and store critical documents, such as passports, in a secure location.

Don't litter: Sardinia has some of the most magnificent natural scenery in Italy. To preserve the beauty of the island, it is critical to properly dispose of rubbish and prevent littering on beaches or in public areas.

Don't assume everyone speaks English: While English is widely spoken in tourist areas, it is not a guarantee that everyone you meet will speak the language. Be patient and try to communicate with locals using simple Italian phrases or a translation software.

Don't go during peak season: Sardinia can get congested during peak tourist season, which is usually from June to August. Consider visiting during the shoulder seasons of May or September, when the weather is still great but the people are lighter.

Don't forget to carry cash: While credit cards are accepted in most locations, it is always a good idea to have some cash on hand for little transactions and to avoid any complications with card readers.

5 Misconception about Sardinia

In this Amazing Chapter, we will address 5 popular misunderstandings about Sardinia and present a comprehensive explanation of the facts.

Sardinia is basically like any other Italian city.
One of the most common misconceptions about Sardinia is that it is just like any other Italian city, with the same food, culture, and way of life. This, however, is not the case. Sardinia is a distinct region with its own culture, traditions, and way of life. Sardinians speak a language distinct from Italian. Sardinian cuisine is also distinct, with typical dishes such as Porceddu (roasted suckling pig), Pane Frattau (a sort of bread with tomato sauce, cheese, and egg), and Carasau (a type of flatbread).

Sardinia is only a beach destination.

Another prevalent myth about Sardinia is that it is solely a beach destination with nothing else to do on the island. While Sardinia has some of the most gorgeous beaches in the world, the island has much more than its shoreline. Sardinia also has a variety of historical sites, including the ancient city of Nora, the medieval city of Alghero, and the UNESCO World Heritage site of Nuraghe Su Nuraxi.

Sardinia is a perilous place.

Many people feel that Sardinia is a dangerous location to visit, with high levels of crime and violence. This, however, is not the case. Sardinia is one of the safest areas in Europe, with low crime rates and a hospitable community. In reality, Sardinia is recognized for its hospitality, and guests are frequently treated like family.

Sardinia is an expensive destination.

Another common myth about Sardinia is that it is an expensive destination to visit, with exorbitant prices for lodging, food, and activities. While some places of Sardinia can be fairly pricy, there are also lots of budget-friendly options. Indeed, Sardinia is an excellent destination for budget travelers, with inexpensive lodging options such as hostels, camping grounds, and guesthouses.

Sardinia is a summer-only location.

Finally, many people feel that Sardinia is only worth visiting during the summer months, and that there is little to see or do the rest of the year. This, however, is not the case. Sardinia is a year-round destination with plenty to see and do no matter what time of year it is. During the winter, visitors can go skiing in the Alps and explore the island's various museums, art galleries, and historical monuments.

Welcome to Sardinia

Welcome to Sardinia, an exquisite island in the midst of the Mediterranean Sea. Sardinia is a beautiful jewel waiting to be discovered, with its rich history, breathtaking landscapes, and distinct culture.

Sardinia is the Mediterranean's second-largest island, located off the western coast of Italy. Its craggy coastline, crystal-clear oceans, and pristine wildlife make it a favorite destination for beachgoers and outdoor enthusiasts alike. Sardinia offers visitors a diverse range of experiences, from the gorgeous beaches of Costa Smeralda to the craggy highlands of Gennargentu National Park.

The Nuraghe, an ancient stone building dating back to the Bronze Age, is one of the island's most famous sights. These ancient remains are strewn around the island and bear witness to the island's rich history and cultural heritage. Visitors can learn more about the island's interesting past by visiting the many archaeological sites and museums.

Sardinia is also recognized for its exquisite cuisine, which is highly inspired by its Mediterranean surroundings. Fresh fish, savory cheeses, and locally grown veggies are just a few of the gastronomic delights guests may anticipate to enjoy throughout their stay. Traditional delicacies such as pane carasau, a thin and crispy flatbread, and malloreddus, a Sardinian pasta, are must-tries for foodies.

Sardinia has various world-class spas and wellness centers for individuals wishing to unwind and relax. The island's natural hot springs and therapeutic mud baths are thought to offer healing characteristics, making them a popular choice for individuals looking to revitalize their body and mind.

Sardinia is recognized for its colorful festivals and celebrations, in addition to its natural beauty and cultural legacy. From the La Festa di San Giovanni in June to the Sagra della Zuppa Gallurese in August, there are numerous events that highlight the island's traditions and customs.

Overall, Sardinia is a must-see destination for anyone wishing to enjoy the beauty and charm of the Mediterranean. With its gorgeous landscapes, rich history, delectable cuisine, and kind hospitality, it's easy to see why Sardinia has become a popular travel destination for people from all over the world. So pack your luggage and prepare to discover the charm of Sardinia for yourself.

When to Go

When arranging a trip to Sardinia, it is critical to consider the season. The climate on the island varies greatly depending on the season, which can impact your overall experience. In this post, we will explore the best time to visit Sardinia for first-time visitors.

Summer (June-August)

Summer is the most popular time to visit Sardinia, and with good reason. The weather is pleasant and sunny, with lengthy daytime hours. The beaches on the island are magnificent, and the waters are ideal for swimming, snorkeling, and other water sports. This is the peak season for travelers from all around the world. This also means that rates for lodgings and activities may rise.

If you plan to visit Sardinia during the summer, it is best to book your lodgings and activities ahead of time to avoid the bother of overbooked hotels and activities. This is especially true if you intend to visit major tourist locations such as Costa Smeralda, Porto Cervo, and Alghero.

Autumn (September-November)

Autumn is a good season to visit Sardinia for first-time visitors who seek a more relaxed experience. The people have dispersed, and the weather is still warm, but not as hot as it was during the summer months. The island is stunning during this time of year, with warm oranges and browns dominating the landscape.

During this time, you can still enjoy the beaches and water sports activities, but with less people around. This is also an excellent time for hiking and discovering the island's natural beauties. The sea is still warm enough for swimming, and visibility is often superb.

Winter (December-February)

The winter in Sardinia is pleasant, although it may be unpredictable, with rain and strong gusts on occasion. Temperatures on the island can drop to around 10°C, however it rarely snows. However, you can still enjoy the island's beauty during this period, albeit from a different vantage point. The terrain is lush and green, and the island's cultural legacy is more accessible, with less visitors.

This is an excellent time to see the island's archeological sites, such as the Nuragic Complex of Barumini or the Tombs of the Giants. You can also enjoy the island's winter celebrations, such as the

Carnival of Oristano, which is noted for its distinctive masks and costumes.

Spring (March-May)

Spring is an ideal season to visit Sardinia for first-time visitors who wish to avoid crowds and appreciate the island's natural beauty. The weather is moderate, with intermittent rains, and the island's vegetation and fauna are in full bloom. This is an excellent season for hiking and exploring the island's magnificent landscapes, such as the Gennargentu National Park.

Because the island is less congested at this season, pricing for lodgings and activities are frequently lower. The sea is still a little cool for swimming, but you can still enjoy the island's beaches and water sports activities.

Getting There

Getting to Sardinia can be difficult for first-time visitors. However, with some careful planning, you can make your trip to this magnificent island as seamless and stress-free as possible. In this post, we will offer you with all of the information you need to get to Sardinia and make the most of your trip.

The first thing to consider while visiting Sardinia is how you will get there. The island has three airports: Cagliari-Elmas Airport in the south, Alghero-Fertilia Airport in the northwest, and Olbia-Costa Smeralda Airport in the northeast. All three airports serve flights from a variety of European locations, including London, Paris, Frankfurt, and Madrid. It is crucial to note, however, that flight schedules and availability can change depending on the season.

The next step is to get to your hotel once you arrive at the airport. If you are staying in one of the island's major cities, such as Cagliari, Alghero, or Olbia, you may easily take a cab or public transportation to your hotel. However, if you intend to explore more remote areas, renting a car may be more convenient. Sardinia has a strong road network, and driving may be a terrific way to experience the island's gorgeous scenery at your own speed.

The optimum time to visit Sardinia is also an important factor. The island is noted for its pleasant Mediterranean environment, with long, sunny summers and mild winters. The peak tourist season is from June through September, when temperatures can exceed 35°C. If you want to avoid crowds, the ideal time to visit Sardinia is in the spring (April to May) or fall (September to October). During these months, the weather remains warm and bright, but crowds are smaller and prices are often lower.

The gorgeous coastline of Sardinia is one of the island's key draws. The island features almost 2,000 kilometers of coastline, with beaches ranging from quiet coves to extensive lengths of golden sand. Costa Smeralda in the northeast, Chia in the south, and Stintino in the northwest are some of the most popular beaches. Many of these beaches can become busy during high tourist season, so it's best to arrive early or visit outside of peak hours.

Aside from its beaches, Sardinia is well-known for its rich cultural legacy. The island has a rich and fascinating history, with influences from the Phoenicians, Carthaginians, Romans, and Arabs. The Nuragic complex of Barumini, a UNESCO World Heritage site, and the ancient city of Tharros, founded by the Phoenicians in the eighth century BC, are two must-see cultural destinations in Sardinia. There are also numerous museums and galleries on the island that showcase Sardinian art, history, and culture.

Sardinia is recognized for its food and wine, in addition to its cultural attractions. The island has a strong culinary culture, with a concentration on fresh, local items like as seafood, pork, cheese, and vegetables. Some must-try foods include culurgiones (stuffed ravioli with potato and cheese), seadas (a cheese and honey dessert), and porceddu (roasted suckling pig). Sardinia also has some good wineries that produce a variety of wines from the island's distinct grape varietals.

Visa Requirements

As a first-time visitor to Sardinia, you should be informed of the visa requirements before making your plans. The visa requirements for Sardinia, Italy, will be covered in this article.

Visa waiver

You do not require a visa to enter Sardinia or any other area of Italy if you are a citizen of the European Union (EU), the European Economic Area (EEA), or Switzerland. You can stay in the nation without a visa for up to 90 days.

Visa Waiver Scheme

You can enter Sardinia or any other area of Italy without a visa if you are a citizen of a nation that is a member of the Visa Waiver Program (VWP). Citizens of the United States, Canada, Australia, Japan, and many other nations are included in the VWP. However, before to your journey, you must apply for an Electronic System for Travel Authorization (ESTA). The ESTA is a $14 online application that must be submitted at least 72 hours before departure.

Visa Schengen

If you are a non-EU, EEA, or Swiss citizen, you will require a Schengen visa to enter Sardinia or any other area of Italy. The Schengen visa permits you to visit any of the 26 Schengen nations, which encompass the majority of Europe. To apply for a Schengen visa, you must go through your home country's Italian embassy or consulate. A valid passport, two passport-sized pictures, travel insurance, and proof of financial resources to finance your stay in Italy are all required for a Schengen visa.

Because the Schengen visa application procedure might take several weeks, it is critical to plan ahead of time and apply as early as possible. The cost of a Schengen visa varies by nationality and length of stay.

Other Conditions

There are certain additional criteria to enter Sardinia or any other part of Italy in addition to the visa requirements. Among these are:

A valid passport: Your passport must be valid for at least three months beyond the period of time you want to spend in Italy.

Proof of lodging: You must provide proof of where you will stay in Italy, such as a hotel reservation or a letter of invitation from a friend or family member.

Proof of return travel is required, such as a round-trip plane ticket.

Sufficient funds: You must have enough money for your stay in Italy, such as a bank statement or a credit card.

Busiest time to visit Sardinia

If this is your first vacation to Sardinia, you may be thinking when is the best time to visit this island paradise.

Sardinia's tourist season runs from June through August. During this season, the island is buzzing with visitors from all over the world, and the beaches, hotels, and restaurants are at their busiest. If you want to experience a lively and active atmosphere, the summer months are the perfect time to visit Sardinia. The island is bustling with activity, and there will be lots of festivals, concerts, and cultural events taking place throughout the season.

However, there are certain drawbacks to visiting Sardinia during the summer months. The island can be highly congested, and you may encounter long lines and wait times at popular attractions. The beaches can also be busy, making it difficult to locate a peaceful location to rest and decompress. Furthermore, the weather can be exceedingly hot and humid, with temperatures frequently exceeding 30°C. If you are not used to being outside for extended periods of time, you may find it uncomfortable.

If you prefer a more tranquil and easygoing atmosphere, spring and fall are the finest times to visit Sardinia. From March to May and September to November, the island is less congested, and the weather is mild and pleasant. During these months, you may enjoy the natural beauty of the island without the crowds, and you can explore the beaches and countryside at your own speed.

During the spring months, the island is covered in a carpet of wildflowers, and the countryside is lush and verdant. This is a terrific time to explore the hiking trails and national parks, and you can experience the splendor of the island's natural surroundings without the crowds. Furthermore, the weather is calm and pleasant, with temperatures averaging around 20°C. The sea is still a little frigid for swimming, but you may enjoy other activities such as kayaking, sailing, and snorkeling.

The island is less populated in the autumn months than in the summer, but the weather remains warm and pleasant. The beaches are less crowded now, and you can find peaceful locations to relax and decompress. Furthermore, the sea is warm and welcoming, and you may swim, sunbathe, and enjoy water sports without the heat and throng of the summer months.

If you want to save money on your trip to Sardinia, the best time to come is during the low season, which runs from December to February. During these months, the island is quiet and tranquil, and you may appreciate the natural beauty of the island without the crowds. However, the weather can be frigid and wet, and many hotels, restaurants, and attractions are closed for the season. If you are ready to suffer the cold and rain, you can discover fantastic prices on flights, hotels, and activities, and you can tour the island on a budget.

Finally, the perfect time to visit Sardinia depends on your own interests and travel style. Summer is the greatest season to visit if you want a lively and active atmosphere. If you want a quieter and more relaxed atmosphere, the spring and autumn months are the finest times to visit. Furthermore, if you want to save money on your trip, the low season is the greatest time to visit, but be prepared for chilly and rainy weather.

Cheapest time to visit

Sardinia, the second-largest island in the Mediterranean Sea, is a popular tourist destination for those wishing to explore its magnificent coastline, rough mountains, and ancient ruins. However, as with any major tourist site, the cost of visiting Sardinia varies substantially depending on the time of year. In this post, we'll look at the best time for travelers to visit Sardinia.

The summer months of June, July, and August are the busiest for tourism in Sardinia. During this season, the island is overrun with tourists from all over the world, and prices for everything from flights to hotels are at their highest. If you want to save money on your trip to Sardinia, avoid going during these months.

The shoulder season, which runs from May through October, can also be expensive. However, if you're willing to visit during the off-season, you can save a large amount of money on your trip.

The winter months of December, January, and February are the most affordable months to visit Sardinia. During this time, the island is much quieter, and many hotels and restaurants may be closed for the season. However, if you're searching for a calm vacation and don't mind the chilly temperature, this can be a terrific time to visit Sardinia.

If you want to visit Sardinia in the spring or fall, the months of March, April, October, and November can provide a decent blend of good weather and inexpensive pricing. During these months, the island is less congested, and costs for lodgings and activities can be significantly lower than during peak season.

When it comes to flights, keep in mind that pricing can vary based on the time of year. Flights to Sardinia are often at their highest during the summer months, so if you want to save money, book your travel during the off-season.

Accommodations can sometimes be more economical during the off-season, especially in smaller towns and villages. During high season, many hotels and resorts may impose a minimum stay of several nights, which can raise the cost of your trip. However, during the off-season, you may be able to discover amazing prices on hotels, bed and breakfasts, and other lodgings.

The cost of activities and attractions can vary substantially depending on what you're interested in.

Many beaches in Sardinia are free to visit, and hiking and visiting the island's many old ruins and archaeological sites can be a fantastic way to save money on your vacation. However, some activities, such as water sports and guided tours, can be rather costly. If you want to save money, study activities ahead of time and plan your itinerary appropriately.

In addition to saving money, visiting Sardinia during the off-season might provide a more authentic experience. During the peak season, many regions of the island might become overwhelmed with tourists, making it difficult to enjoy the actual culture and way of life of the Sardinian people. However, during the off-season, you may have the opportunity to engage with residents and learn more about the island's culture.

Finally, the best time to visit Sardinia for tourists is during the winter months of December, January, and

February. However, if you want to strike a balance between nice weather and low pricing, the months of March, April, October, and November are all excellent choices. You may save a lot of money on your vacation to Sardinia by planning ahead of time and completing your homework.

Foreign Transactional Fee

As a well-liked travel location for foreigners, there are several fees that guests should be aware of, like international transaction fees.

A cost that is added to a credit card transaction when a purchase is made in a currency other than the card's native currency is known as a foreign transaction fee. Usually between 2 and 5 percent of the entire transaction cost, this charge is calculated as a percentage of the purchase price.

Foreign transaction fees can be imposed to a variety of transactions made in Sardinia, including travel charges, restaurant tabs, travel costs, and lodging expenses. It is crucial that travelers are aware of these charges and include them in their travel budget overall.

There are various options for visitors to Sardinia to avoid or reduce international transaction fees. Utilizing a credit card that has no foreign transaction fees is one choice. It is worthwhile to contact your bank or credit card issuer before flying as many credit cards now provide this perk.

Using cash for transactions wherever possible is an additional choice. Even though this might not be practical for bigger expenditures like hotel stays, it can be a decent alternative for smaller costs like lunches and trinkets. Additionally, tourists should be aware that some shops might give a discount if cash is used, which can help offset any fees associated with international transactions.

Finally, visitors may want to think about using a currency exchange agency to convert their home currency into euros before flying to Sardinia. Even though there may be a cost involved, doing this can help reduce foreign transaction costs for credit card transactions.

Visitors to Sardinia should be aware of additional fees that could be charged when using credit cards in addition to foreign transaction fees. on instance, certain retailers may levy a premium on credit card purchases that might be as much as 5% of the total.

Important to keep in mind is that while the majority of businesses in Sardinia take credit cards, there may be a few smaller businesses that only accept cash.

Therefore, it is a wise idea to always have some cash on you when moving about the island.

Top 5 best places For Shopping

Sardinia is a fantastic place to shop, with a large selection of traditional and contemporary goods that showcase the island's distinct culture and history. The top 5 tourist-friendly shopping locations in Sardinia will be covered in this post.

Cagliari

Shopping fans should visit Cagliari, the capital of Sardinia. It provides a diverse selection of stores and boutiques to suit every taste and price range. Via Roma, Cagliari's busiest retail avenue, is lined with upscale clothing boutiques, jewelry stores, and specialty shops. The San Benedetto Market in Cagliari is another fantastic site to buy. Here, you can discover seasonal produce, fish, fruits, and cheese in addition to other typical Sardinian goods like bread, wine, and cheese.

Alghero

Another excellent location for shopping is Alghero, a quaint medieval town on Sardinia's northwest coast. The old town of Alghero is a labyrinth of winding lanes and alleyways dotted with artisanal stores selling textiles, ceramics, and jewelry. In Alghero, Via Carlo Alberto is the busiest shopping route. Here, you can discover a variety of businesses that sell apparel, shoes, and accessories.

Olbia

Olbia, a bustling town on Sardinia's northeast coast, is a fantastic place to shop. There are many different stores and boutiques there that sell clothes, shoes, and accessories in addition to typical Sardinian goods like olive oil, honey, and wine. Corso Umberto, the main shopping district of Olbia, is lined with upscale clothing boutiques, jewelry stores, and specialty shops.

In Porto Cervo

Shopping for fine goods is a delight at Porto Cervo, a posh resort town on Sardinia's northeast coast. It is the location of the most prestigious designer outlets, such as Prada, Gucci, and Louis Vuitton. Via della Chiesa, the main thoroughfare for shopping in Porto Cervo, is surrounded by upscale stores that sell apparel, accessories, and shoes.

Nuoro

Nuoro, a town in central Sardinia, is a terrific place to go for authentic Sardinian shopping. There are numerous artisanal shops and studios there where you can buy authentic Sardinian goods including jewelry, ceramics, and textiles. Corso Garibaldi, Nuoro's busiest shopping avenue, is lined with artisanal shops selling handcrafted goods.

II. Planning Your Trip

Itinerary Plan

If you're a first-time visitor to Sardinia, a well-planned itinerary will help you explore the island's various attractions and have a great vacation. Here's a seven-day itinerary to help you make the most of your stay on the island.

Day 1: Arrival in Cagliari

Take some time after landing at Cagliari International Airport to rest and adjust to the local climate. Explore the city's historical heart, Castello, which is set on a hill overlooking the sea. The area's tiny streets, modest squares, and antique churches make it the ideal site to experience Sardinia's rich history and culture. You can also visit the National Archaeological Museum of Cagliari, which houses an extraordinary collection of antiquities from the Nuragic culture.

Day 2: Chia Beach Exploration

On the second day, go to Chia, a village in southern Sardinia with some of the island's most magnificent beaches. The white sands and turquoise waters of Chia's beaches are incredibly gorgeous, making it an ideal day vacation destination. Among the beaches to visit are Su Giudeu, Tuerredda, and Sa Colonia. You can also attempt water sports such as kayaking, windsurfing, and snorkeling.

Day 3: Discover Alghero

Visit the lovely village of Alghero on the northwest coast of Sardinia on day three. The town is noted for its Catalan architecture and is an excellent place to learn about Sardinia's history and culture. While at Alghero, you can tour the old town, walk along the ramparts, and see the Gothic-style Alghero Cathedral. You may also take a stroll around the waterfront, take in the breathtaking vistas, and sample some of the town's delectable seafood cuisine.

Day 4: Visit the Nuraghe di Barumini

On the fourth day, see the Nuraghe di Barumini, a UNESCO World Heritage Site in the center of Sardinia. The location is home to several well-preserved Nuraghe, which are ancient stone structures created during the Nuragic culture. Learn about the island's rich history and culture, as well as how the Nuragic civilisation evolved over time.

Day 5: Exploring the Costa Smeralda

On the fifth day, go to the Costa Smeralda, a magnificent length of coastline in northern Sardinia. Here, you may enjoy the crystal-clear seas, white sands, and breathtaking views of the sea. You can also go to Porto Cervo, which is famed for its luxury yachts and high-end boutiques.

Day 6: Trekking in the Gennargentu National Park

On day six, visit the Gennargentu National Park in central Sardinia. The park contains some of the most spectacular natural features on the island, including mountains, woods, and lakes. You may enjoy the breathtaking environment by hiking, trekking, or mountain biking here.

Day 7: Relaxing in La Maddalena

On the final day of your Sardinia trip, visit La Maddalena, a small island off Sardinia's northeastern coast. Relax on the island's beautiful beaches, swim in the crystal-clear waters, and savor the native food. You can also take a boat tour to visit the surrounding islands, which are noted for their spectacular beauty and clean waters.

Overall, this seven-day trip will give you a taste of Sardinia's many attractions, from its magnificent beaches to its rich cultural legacy and natural beauty. However, there are many more locations to visit on the island, and if you have more time, you may add other destinations to your schedule, such as the ancient remains of Tharros or the picturesque town of Bosa.

When planning a trip to Sardinia, keep in mind that the best time to visit is during the summer months, from June to September, when the weather is warm and sunny and the beaches are at their best. It's also a good idea to rent a car to explore the island at your own leisure, as public transportation can be limited in some locations.

There are numerous lodging alternatives available, ranging from luxury resorts to budget-friendly motels and guesthouses. Popular spots to stay include the Costa Smeralda, Alghero, and Cagliari, but there are also many attractive towns and villages dotted throughout the island that offer a more real experience.

Mode of Exchange in Sardinia

The style of exchange practiced on the island is a particularly fascinating component of this civilization. Unlike many other parts of the world, Sardinia maintains a distinct trade system based on a blend of bartering and monetary transactions.

The "barter system" is a popular means of exchange in Sardinia. This system is centered on the trade of products and services between individuals without the use of money. For example, a farmer would exchange a portion of his crops for the services of a carpenter in erecting a fence. This form of transaction is especially common in rural sections of the island, where people still have strong ties to traditional ways of life.

The "family economy" is another popular style of commerce in Sardinia. This approach is founded on the concept of pooling resources and sharing products and services among family members. For example, if one family member owns a vineyard, they may share their wine with other family members in exchange for other commodities or services. This form of trade is especially popular in locations where families have lived for generations and there is a strong sense of community.

While these ancient ways of exchange are still popular in many regions of the island, tourists can still engage in more traditional types of commerce. For example, across Sardinia, there are several shops and markets where visitors can use cash to purchase a wide range of goods and services. These stores and marketplaces sell anything from handcrafted products and souvenirs to local fruit and wine.

In addition to these more traditional kinds of commerce, there are a variety of unique chances for tourists to firsthand experience Sardinia's manner of exchange. Throughout the year, for example, there are numerous festivals and fairs where tourists can engage in traditional forms of bartering and trading. These activities provide an insight into the island's rich cultural history as well as an opportunity to interact with locals in a meaningful way.

One particularly noteworthy example is the "Sa Sartiglia" event, which takes place in the town of Oristano. This festival is based on a historic method of horseback riding used by knights in medieval times. During the festival, riders dress in traditional costumes and execute elaborate horsemanship movements in front of large crowds of residents and tourists. In addition to horseback riding, guests to the event can engage in traditional forms of bargaining and commerce.

Another example of a one-of-a-kind mechanism of exchange in Sardinia is the "wine tasting tour." Many local wineries provide tours and tastings where visitors can sample a range of wines and learn about the winemaking process. In many cases, visitors can also purchase bottles of wine directly from the winery, allowing them to engage in a more personal kind of trade with the local community.

Overall, the mode of exchange in Sardinia is a unique blend of ancient and modern modes of commerce. While bartering and family economies are still prominent in many regions of the island, travelers can still engage in more traditional types of commerce including cash. Additionally, there are a number of unique possibilities for visitors to engage with locals and experience Sardinia's rich cultural history through festivals, tours, and tastings. Whether you are interested in traditional modes of transaction or more conventional types of commerce, Sardinia has a plethora of possibilities to study and experience its distinctive culture and history.

Where to Stay

Deborah and Peter had been preparing their trip to Sardinia for months, and one of the most essential decisions they had to make was where to stay. They had heard that Sardinia was a magnificent destination with crystal-clear waters and lovely beaches, and they wanted to make sure they chose the appropriate hotel to make their stay unforgettable.

They finally decided on two possibilities after careful research: a magnificent five-star hotel on the Costa Smeralda and a quaint bed & breakfast in the countryside. They decided to book both locations and spend a few days in each to compare their experiences and decide which one they preferred.

Their first stop was a hotel in Costa Smeralda, one of Sardinia's most exclusive locations. They were blown away by the beauty of the place the moment they arrived. The hotel was built on a hill overlooking the bay, and the views were spectacular. The staff greeted them cheerfully and led them to their accommodation, which was big and nicely designed. The accommodation featured a balcony with a view of the sea, and they could hear the waves smashing on the shore.

The hotel has all of the amenities one would expect from a five-star hotel, including a spa, a gym, a swimming pool, and multiple restaurants. Deborah and Peter opted to begin their vacation with a peaceful massage at the spa, and it was divine. The masseuses were professional, and the ambiance was tranquil and peaceful. They went swimming and sunbathing in the pool after the massage.

That evening, they dined at one of the hotel's restaurants, which provided delectable seafood dishes. The service was excellent, and the wine list was broad. They sipped a bottle of local Vermentino while savoring the scenery of the bay.

They decided to explore the region around the hotel the next day. They took a boat ride to the nearby islands, which were breathtaking. The water was so pure that they could see the fish swimming beneath them, and the beaches were immaculate. They spent the day sunning, swimming, and snorkeling, and they even saw some dolphins on the way back.

They agreed to have dinner at a local restaurant outside the hotel in the evening. They sampled some classic Sardinian meals, such as culurgiones (a sort of ravioli filled with potato and mint) and porceddu (roasted suckling pig). The cuisine was great, and the restaurant had a pleasant and authentic ambiance.

Deborah and Peter checked out of the hotel after two days and went to a bed and breakfast in the countryside. The B&B was in a little community surrounded by rolling hills and vineyards. The owners greeted them kindly and led them to their rustic and wonderful room. The accommodation included a little balcony with a view of the village plaza.

The B&B included a pleasant living room with a fireplace where guests could relax and read. Deborah and Peter spent most of their time in a little garden with a pool. The pool was not as large as the one at the hotel, but it was nice and they had it all to themselves.

Every morning, the B&B's owners offered a delectable breakfast of fresh pastries, homemade jams, and local cheeses. They also advised some nearby activities and eateries, which Deborah and Peter followed.

They went to a nearby winery and tasted some wonderful Cannonau wine, one of Sardinia's most recognized wines. They also visited some of the little communities in the vicinity, which were rich in character and history.

They dined at a small trattoria that featured traditional Sardinian meals. They tasted dishes they had never heard of before, such as malloreddus (a type of gnocchi made with semolina flour and saffron) and seadas (a dessert made with fried dough, cheese, and honey). The cuisine was simple but tasty, and the rates were really affordable.

On their last day at the B&B, the proprietors invited them to a typical Sardinian celebration in a nearby village. The festival was called "Sagra della

Raviola" and it celebrated the local specialty dish of ravioli. They had the opportunity to sample many types of homemade ravioli with various contents and sauces. The event had a lively atmosphere, with live music and dancing, and Deborah and Peter felt they were experiencing true Sardinian culture.

Deborah and Peter had to choose an accomodation after four days in Sardinia. The hotel in Costa Smeralda has a lovely location and great amenities, but it was also very pricey, and they felt a little alienated from the local culture. The B&B in the countryside was less expensive, and it provided them the opportunity to explore the surrounding area and learn about Sardinian culture. In the end, they determined that the B&B provided a more authentic and immersive experience.

Their journey to Sardinia was a terrific experience that taught them that there are many different ways to travel and enjoy a destination. The most luxury and expensive option is not always the best, and it is worth investigating numerous types of lodging to discover the one that best meets your interests and budget. Sardinia is a lovely place with a rich history, culture, and food that is well worth visiting at least once in a lifetime.

What to Pack

Sardinia is a lovely island in the Mediterranean Sea off the coast of Italy. Its crystal-clear waters, white sandy beaches, and magnificent sceneries attract people from all over the world. If you're going to Sardinia, make sure you prepare correctly for the weather and activities you'll be doing. In this post, we'll discuss what to pack for tourists in Sardinia, including advice from Deborah and Peter.

Clothing: Sardinia is recognized for its pleasant and sunny weather, particularly in the summer. Pack shirts, shorts, dresses, and skirts made of cotton or linen that are lightweight and breathable. It's also a good idea to bring along some comfortable walking shoes for visiting the island's many beaches and hiking paths. Sandals or flip flops are ideal for beach days, but bring closed-toe shoes if you intend to perform any difficult excursions or explore rough terrain.

Deborah and Peter, a British couple who recently visited Sardinia, advise taking a light sweater or jacket for chilly evenings, especially if you want to spend time along the seaside. They also recommend taking a hat and sunglasses to protect yourself from the harsh Mediterranean sun.

Swimwear: With so many beautiful beaches to pick from, bring lots of swimwear on your trip to Sardinia. Pack a few different swimsuits to flip between during your visit. Deborah and Peter advise bringing a cover-up or sarong to wear over your swimsuit when walking to and from the beach or stopping for lunch at a local café.

Sun protection: The Mediterranean sun may be harsh, especially between 11 a.m. and 3 p.m. Pack a high-SPF sunscreen and reapply it throughout the day. In case of sunburn, Deborah and Peter recommend bringing after-sun lotion or aloe vera gel.

Electronics: Don't forget to bring your camera or smartphone to record all of the breathtaking vistas and experiences during your trip to Sardinia. Bring charging cables as well as adaptors for any international outlets. Deborah and Peter advise bringing a portable charger with you in case your phone battery expires while you're out exploring.

Medical Supplies: It's usually a good idea to bring a modest first-aid kit, including any prescription prescriptions, when traveling. Deborah and Peter recommend bringing insect repellent and anti-itch lotion in case of mosquito or other bug bites. If you plan on taking any boat tours or ferries, they also recommend having motion sickness medication.

Other necessities: Bring a reusable water bottle to stay hydrated throughout the day, especially if you'll be spending time outside in the hot Mediterranean sun. Deborah and Peter also recommend bringing a small backpack or day bag with you when you go exploring to carry essentials like sunscreen, food, and drink.

Deborah and Peter recommend carrying a few specific items based on their own experience in Sardinia in addition to the above requirements. They recommend bringing a good book or two to read on the beach or during downtime. They also advise carrying a portable Bluetooth speaker to listen to music on the beach or at your lodging. Finally, they recommend bringing a deck of cards or other little games for evenings spent inside or on rainy days.

Hotel and Resort

One of Sardinia's biggest draws are its magnificent hotels and resorts, which provide a high degree of comfort, superb services, and stunning views of the island's coastline. In this post, we will look at some of the top hotels and resorts in Sardinia and what they have to offer.

The Hotel Cala di Volpe in Porto Cervo is one of Sardinia's most well-known hotels. This luxury hotel is built to look like a typical fishing town and is located on a hilltop overlooking the Mediterranean Sea. The hotel features 121 rooms and suites, each designed in a traditional Sardinian style with handcrafted furniture and textiles. The hotel offers a private beach, three swimming pools, a fitness center, and a spa.

The Forte Village Resort, located on Sardinia's southern shore, is another popular hotel. This resort is nestled amid 116 acres of manicured gardens and offers a variety of amenities, including hotel rooms, suites, villas, and apartments. The resort offers a private beach, many swimming pools, and a variety of recreational facilities, including tennis courts, a football pitch, and a golf course. The resort also boasts a wide variety of restaurants, pubs, and cafes serving everything from classic Italian food to foreign fare.

The Hotel Romazzino, also located in Porto Cervo, is a good choice for those seeking a more quiet and intimate experience. This hotel has only 100 rooms and suites, each decorated in a contemporary Sardinian style with natural materials and soothing colors. The hotel features a private beach, a swimming pool, a fitness center, and a spa, as well as a variety of restaurants and bars providing gourmet cuisine and great wines.

Another popular option for visitors searching for a deluxe hotel in Sardinia is the La Maddalena Hotel and Yacht Club. This hotel is located on the island of La Maddalena, just off the coast of Sardinia, and offers breathtaking views of the Mediterranean Sea. The hotel features 33 rooms and suites, each furnished in a basic and beautiful style with natural materials and colors. The hotel features a private beach, a swimming pool, a spa, and a variety of restaurants and bars serving delectable Mediterranean cuisine.

Finally, for those seeking a more traditional Sardinian experience, the Hotel Su Gologone is a wonderful choice. This hotel sits in the centre of the island, surrounded by the picturesque Supramonte Mountains. The hotel features 68 rooms and suites, each designed in a traditional Sardinian style with handcrafted furniture and textiles. The hotel offers a swimming pool, a fitness center, and a spa, as well as a restaurant serving outstanding Sardinian cuisine.

To summarize, Sardinia is a gorgeous island with some of the top hotels and resorts in Italy. Sardinia has something for everyone, whether you're seeking for a magnificent beach resort or a hidden mountain getaway. So, plan your next vacation to Sardinia and experience the beauty and grandeur of this lovely island.

Budget Friendly Accomodations

Sardinia is a magnificent Mediterranean island that draws visitors from all over the world due to its crystal-clear waters, breathtaking beaches, and natural beauty. However, due to the enormous number of tourists, the island can become rather expensive, particularly in terms of accommodation. But don't be alarmed! There are still budget-friendly lodging options on the island, and this article will look at some of the best.

Hostels Hostels are a terrific alternative for budget tourists, and Sardinia offers some fantastic ones. They provide shared dormitory-style dormitories or private rooms at reasonable prices. Some of the top hostels in Sardinia include the Alghero Hostel and the Hostel Marina in Cagliari. Both are clean, safe, and in good locations.

Bed and Breakfasts

Bed & breakfasts are another fantastic option for low-cost lodging in Sardinia. Many bed and breakfasts provide a more personalized experience than hotels, and they are frequently located in old buildings that add to the attractiveness of the visit. The Affittacamere Art Rooms in Alghero and the B&B Le Pavoncelle in Cagliari are two of the top-rated bed and breakfasts in Sardinia.

Agriturismos are farm stays that provide visitors with a one-of-a-kind experience. They offer a more authentic view of Sardinian life and are frequently less expensive than hotels. Visitors can stay in rural locations, surrounded by nature and the island's traditional agriculture. Agriturismo La Quercia in Olbia and Agriturismo Su Recreu in Oristano are two of the best in Sardinia.

Camping is a wonderful budget-friendly choice for individuals who like the great outdoors. Sardinia offers various campgrounds, some of which are in spectacular natural settings. Camping also allows you to meet other people and enjoy the natural beauty of the island. Camping Village Laguna Blu in Alghero and Camping Cala Gonone in Dorgali are two of Sardinia's top campsites.

Guest Houses Guest houses are modest, family-run establishments that provide a homey vibe. They are frequently positioned in residential areas, providing a look into local life. Guesthouses are typically less expensive than hotels and provide a more authentic experience. The Antica Dimora del Gruccione in Santu Lussurgiu and the Domu Antiga in Nuoro are two of Sardinia's top-rated guest houses.

Apartments

Renting an apartment is a terrific method to save money on lodging, especially for families or parties. Apartments provide a more spacious and private stay, and they frequently include a kitchen, which is perfect for cooking meals and saving money on eating out. Popular booking services like Airbnb and HomeAway have some of the greatest apartments in Sardinia.

Budget Hotels

Budget hotels are an excellent choice for folks who want a private room but do not want to break the bank. While they may not have all of the amenities of a luxury hotel, they do give a comfortable stay at a lesser cost. Some of the top affordable hotels in Sardinia include the Hotel Mistral in Alghero and the Hotel Miramare in Cagliari.

To summarize, Sardinia is a lovely island with plenty of budget-friendly lodging options for visitors. There is something to meet everyone's needs and preferences, from hostels to farm stays, camping to guest houses. Visitors can save money on accommodation by selecting one of these low-cost options, and then use those savings to explore the island's many activities and experiences.

Luxurious Accomodations in Sardinia

Tourists in Sardinia have a plethora of options for upscale hotels. Sardinia has a variety of lodgings to suit all types of guests, from magnificent villas to luxurious resorts.

Staying in a luxury villa is one of the greatest ways to experience Sardinia. The island is home to some of the most spectacular villas with breathtaking views of the sea and surrounding scenery. These villas have all of the latest conveniences, such as private pools, gardens, and large living rooms. Many of these villas are located in exclusive gated communities and provide complete privacy and security.

The home del Parco and Spa is one such magnificent home in Sardinia. It is situated in the heart of the

Costa Smeralda and is surrounded by lush green gardens and stunning sea views. The estate has big rooms and suites, each designed in a distinct and exquisite way. The property also has a private beach, a spa, and a fitness facility. Guests can also dine in the on-site restaurant, which serves traditional Italian food.

A resort is another popular alternative for premium accommodations in Sardinia. The island is home to some of Europe's most opulent resorts, which provide a variety of amenities and services to suit all types of guests. The resorts have private beaches, swimming pools, spas, and restaurants, making them the ideal place to relax and unwind.

The Forte Village Resort is one such magnificent resort in Sardinia. It is located on the island's southern coast and has 47 hectares of breathtaking scenery. The resort offers a variety of lodgings, including suites, bungalows, and villas, each furnished in a distinct and exquisite style. The resort also has a private beach, a spa, a fitness center, and a variety of sports facilities. Guests can also dine at the resort's 21 restaurants, which provide a variety of international and local cuisines.

Staying in a traditional farmhouse or a historic villa is an ideal alternative for people who want to experience Sardinia's real charm. These lodgings provide a one-of-a-kind and authentic experience, allowing guests to immerse themselves in the island's rich cultural past. Many of these farmhouses and villas have been meticulously refurbished to provide modern facilities while retaining their original characteristics and character.

The Villa Sant'Andrea is one such historic farmhouse in Sardinia. It is set in the picturesque countryside, surrounded by olive orchards and vineyards. The farmhouse has big rooms and suites that are all designed in a traditional Sardinian style. Guests can also take advantage of a variety of amenities, such as a private pool, a spa, and a restaurant serving authentic Sardinian cuisine.

Finally, Sardinia has a variety of exquisite accommodations to suit all types of guests. Sardinia has it all, whether you're searching for a magnificent villa with stunning sea views, a resort with all the modern conveniences, or a traditional farmhouse. Sardinia, with its breathtaking scenery, crystal-clear waters, and rich cultural heritage, is the ideal destination for a sumptuous vacation.

How to make friends with the locals

The possibility to make friends with the people is one of the most gratifying experiences for visitors to this beautiful island. Sardinians are a warm, hospitable people who are proud of their culture and traditions. Here are some pointers on how to make friends with the people in Sardinia.

Learn some Italian phrases.
While many Sardinians know English, it's always a good idea to learn a few Italian words to help you converse with the locals. Not only will this make it easier to travel around and order food, but it will also demonstrate that you are making an effort to learn about their culture. Some important phrases to know include "ciao" (hello), "grazie" (thank you), and "mi chiamo" (my name is).

Attend local events.

Sardinia hosts a number of festivals and events throughout the year, including the Sagra del Redentore in Nuoro and the Festa di Sant'Efisio in Cagliari. Attending these events is a terrific opportunity to immerse yourself in the local culture and meet new people. You can also go to local markets, concerts, and other events to meet others who share your interests.

Join a sports club or group.

If you enjoy sports, joining a local sports club or group is a terrific way to meet new people. Sardinia is home to a number of sports clubs, including football, basketball, and volleyball teams. There are also groups for hiking, cycling, and other outdoor hobbies. Joining an organization or club will not only help you make friends, but it will also allow you to explore the island's beautiful natural beauty.

Volunteer

Volunteering is an excellent way to give back to the community while also making new acquaintances. Volunteer possibilities on Sardinia include environmental projects, animal shelters, and community organizations. You can also volunteer on local farms and learn about sustainable agriculture by joining organizations such as WWOOF (World Wide Opportunities on Organic Farms).

Take a culinary class.

Food is an important aspect of Sardinian culture, and attending a cooking class is a terrific way to learn about local ingredients and cooking skills. Many cooking workshops are given by locals who are passionate about their food, and they frequently include a supper with new acquaintances. You can also go to local markets and food festivals to taste new foods and meet other foodies.

Stay with a local.

If you really want to immerse yourself in the local culture, consider living with a local host through sites like Couchsurfing or Airbnb. This will allow you to experience daily life in Sardinia and learn about the island's traditions and customs from someone who knows it best. Your host may also introduce you to their friends and family, providing you the opportunity to meet new people.

Be open and pleasant.

Above all, the key to establishing friends with locals in Sardinia is to be open and kind. Smile, be respectful, and show an interest in their culture and way of life. Don't be scared to strike up a conversation with someone you meet on the street or in a café. You never know where it will lead!

Finally, establishing friends with locals in Sardinia is a terrific opportunity to learn about the island's culture and make long-lasting ties. By learning some

Italian phrases, attending local events, joining a sports club or organization, volunteering, taking a cooking lesson, staying with a local, and being open and nice, you'll be well on your way to making new friends and creating amazing memories on this lovely island.

III. Exploring Sardinia

Cagliari

Cagliari, located on the southern coast of the island of Sardinia, is a lovely city with a rich history and culture that any first-time traveller should explore. It has a population of over 160,000 people, making it the largest city on the island and the capital of the Sardinian region.

The gorgeous coastline will be the first thing you notice when you arrive in Cagliari. The city is built on a hill, and its landscape spans from white sandy beaches to craggy cliffs. The beaches are popular tourist destinations, with crystal-clear waters and pleasant temperatures ideal for swimming, sunbathing, and water sports.

The city's ancient town, known as Castello, is a must-see for first-time visitors. It sits atop a hill and is surrounded by medieval-era walls. The streets are tiny and twisting, with many colorful dwellings and old structures. Several cathedrals, museums, and galleries showcase the city's rich history and culture.

The Cathedral of Santa Maria is a well-known landmark in Cagliari. This 13th-century cathedral is located in the middle of the old town and offers a remarkable combination of Romanesque, Gothic, and Baroque architectural styles. Its bell tower provides spectacular views of the city and the surrounding shoreline.

Cagliari's National Archaeological Museum is a must-see for history buffs. The museum is located in the ancient town and displays items from the prehistoric Nuragic civilisation that formerly populated the island. The exhibits include ceramics, jewelry, and tools, all of which provide fascinating insight into the island's history.

Foodies will appreciate touring the city's various restaurants and cafes, which serve a variety of traditional Sardinian specialties. Must-try foods include pane carasau (crispy flatbread), malloreddus (Sardinian gnocchi), and sebadas (fried cheese pastries).

Poetto Beach is another renowned Cagliari site. This eight-kilometer-long beach is a popular location for both locals and tourists. It's the ideal place to unwind, sunbathe, and gaze out over the Mediterranean Sea.

Overall, Cagliari is a lovely city with a lot to offer first-time visitors. From its magnificent coastline and beaches to its rich history and culture, there is something for everyone to enjoy. Cagliari is a must-see destination for anybody interested in visiting the city's ancient ruins, experiencing traditional Sardinian cuisine, or simply relaxing on the beach.

Alghero

Alghero is a lovely beach town on the northwest coast of Sardinia, Italy. Alghero, known for its beautiful beaches, medieval old town, and rich cultural legacy, is an excellent choice for first-time visitors. Here are some of the best things to see and do in Alghero:

The Old Town: Alghero's old town is a tangle of narrow, twisting streets and alleyways dotted with colorful buildings, restaurants, cafes, and stores. It's an excellent spot to walk about and learn about the town's history and culture. The old town is protected by medieval walls that provide stunning views of the sea and harbour.

The Cathedral of Santa Maria is one of Alghero's most recognizable landmarks. The cathedral, built in the Catalan-Gothic style in the 16th century, has a lovely bell tower and a stunning rose window. The cathedral is located in the heart of the old town and is a must-see for any first-time visitor.

The Neptune's Grotto: The Neptune's Grotto is a stunning grotto located on the Capo Caccia peninsula, just a few kilometers from Alghero. The cave is loaded with spectacular rock formations, underground lakes, and a lovely beach. Visitors can enter the cave by a steep staircase built into the cliff and enjoy a guided tour of the cave's interior.

The beaches: Alghero has some of Sardinia's most gorgeous beaches. The most famous of these is the Lido di Alghero, a large expanse of white sand beach just a short walk from the old town. Other popular beaches in the vicinity are Maria Pia, Bombarde, and Mugoni, all of which are easily accessible by public transportation or car.

Alghero is famous for its wonderful cuisine, which combines traditional Sardinian recipes with Catalan and Italian influences. Some must-try delicacies are the fregola, a sort of pasta eaten with shellfish, the porceddu, a roasted suckling pig, and the seadas, a sweet pastry packed with cheese and honey. Alghero has numerous outstanding restaurants, ranging from simple trattorias to premium fine-dining venues.

The Nuraghe Palmavera: The Nuraghe Palmavera is an old megalithic construction located within a few kilometers from Alghero. The Bronze Age construction consists of multiple towers and chambers enclosed by a defensive wall. Visitors can take a guided tour of the site and learn about the history and culture of the Nuragic civilization that once occupied the island.

To summarize, Alghero is an excellent choice for first-time visitors. Alghero has something for everyone, whether you're interested in history, culture, or simply relaxing on the beach. Alghero will leave a lasting impression on any visitor with its gorgeous ancient town, stunning beaches, wonderful cuisine, and rich cultural legacy.

Sassari

Sassari is a lovely city in Sardinia, Italy. With a population of about 130,000 people, it is the island's second largest city. Sassari is a popular tourist destination because of its rich history, culture, and gorgeous architecture.

A walking tour of Sassari's old core is one of the greatest ways to see the city. Many exquisite buildings can be found in this neighborhood, notably the 16th-century Duomo di Sassari, which has a breathtaking Baroque façade and includes notable works of art. The Palazzo Ducale, which was previously the residence of the Dukes of Sassari, and the Fontana di Rosello, a magnificent fountain in Piazza d'Italia, are two more notable structures in the historic center.

The Museo Nazionale Giovanni Antonio Sanna is yet another must-see sight in Sassari. This museum is dedicated to Sardinia's history and culture, and it has an amazing collection of art, antiquities, and archaeological finds. A huge collection of traditional Sardinian costumes and a section dedicated to the Nuragic culture, which flourished on the island during the Bronze Age, are highlights of the museum.

Sassari has a multitude of outstanding specimens from many times for anyone interested in architecture. Aside from the Duomo and Palazzo Ducale, visitors should also see the Church of Santa Maria di Betlem, a stunning Baroque church erected in the 17th century, and the neoclassical Teatro Civico, built in the early 19th century.

Sassari also has a lot to offer foodies. The city is well-known for its delectable cuisine, which includes regional delicacies like pane carasau (a thin, crispy flatbread) and culurgiones (a sort of pasta filled with potato and mint). Visitors should also sample some of the region's wines, such as Cannonau and Vermentino.

Finally, people wishing to enjoy some sun and lovely beaches should head to the surrounding coast. Sassari is only a short drive away from some of Sardinia's most beautiful beaches, including Stintino and the famous La Pelosa Beach, which features crystal-clear waters and breathtaking views.

Overall, Sassari is an enthralling place that has something for every type of traveler. Whether you're interested in history, culture, architecture, food, or nature, this charming Sardinian city has a lot to offer.

Olbia

Olbia is a lovely city on the northeastern coast of the Italian island of Sardinia. It is a renowned tourist destination noted for its natural beauty, historical landmarks, and delectable cuisine. If you're visiting Olbia for the first time, there's much to see and do. Here are some ideas to help you make the most of your trip.

The old city center should be one of your first stops in Olbia. A tangle of narrow streets and alleyways packed with colorful buildings and lovely cafes awaits you here. Take a tour around Piazza Matteotti, the city's largest square, which is surrounded by historic buildings and monuments. The Chiesa di San Paolo, a beautiful church built in the 18th century, is one of the square's most noteworthy structures.

Another must-see in Olbia is the Basilica di San Simplicio, an outstanding 11th-century basilica. The church has a beautiful Romanesque exterior and an exquisite interior with intricate murals and sculptures. It is regarded as one of the most important religious sites on the island and is a popular attraction for both tourists and locals.

If you're interested in history, you should also pay a visit to the Museo Archeologico di Olbia, which displays a fascinating collection of artifacts from the ancient Nuragic civilisation that formerly occupied Sardinia. The museum is housed in the ancient town hall and has exhibits that span the island's history from prehistoric times to the Roman period.

Olbia never disappoints when it comes to nature. A boat excursion around the magnificent islands of the La Maddalena Archipelago is one of the greatest ways to see the area's natural splendor. The crystal-clear waters and white sand beaches of this gorgeous location are incredibly breathtaking, and the islands themselves are home to a variety of diverse flora and fauna.

Olbia is a foodie's dream. The city is well-known for its fresh seafood, traditional Sardinian cuisine, and delectable wines. Make sure to try some of the local specialties, such as the famed culurgiones, a type of stuffed pasta, and porceddu, roasted suckling pig.

Finally, if you want to unwind, visit one of the city's numerous gorgeous beaches. Pittulongu beach, with its soft sand and sparkling sea, is one of the most popular. Check out the beach at Cala Brandinchi, which is known as the "Caribbean of Sardinia" due to its turquoise ocean and pristine beaches.

Finally, Olbia is a lovely and diversified city with something for everyone. Olbia is a place worth exploring if you are interested in history, wildlife, food, or simply soaking up the Mediterranean sun. With its picturesque streets, breathtaking landmarks, and beautiful beaches, you're guaranteed to enjoy a wonderful experience in this area of Sardinia.

Costa Smeralda

Costa Smeralda, located in the northern section of the Italian island of Sardinia, is a renowned tourist destination noted for its magnificent beaches, crystal-clear waters, and opulent resorts. There's enough to see for travelers visiting the area, with its stunning scenery, lively towns, and rich cultural legacy. In this article, we'll look at some of the best things to do in Costa Smeralda.

The beaches are the main draw of Costa Smeralda, and there are plenty to pick from. Cala Granu, a quiet cove with crystal-clear waters surrounded by rugged cliffs, is one of the most well-known. The beach is ideal for swimming and sunbathing, and there are numerous amenities available, such as sun loungers, umbrellas, and beach bars.

Spiaggia del Principe, with its silky, white sand and turquoise waves, is another must-see beach. This beach is likewise bordered by rocks and trees, giving it an isolated and natural feel. To explore the area, visitors can rent paddle boats or go along the neighboring walking pathways.

In addition to the beaches, Costa Smeralda offers a variety of other outdoor activities. Hiking is a popular sport in the area, and there are various paths that provide spectacular views of the shoreline and neighboring landscapes. The Path of the Giants is a popular hike that leads hikers through an ancient cork forest.

For those who like aquatic activities, there are several chances for snorkeling, scuba diving, and even sailing. The beautiful waters of Costa Smeralda are home to a variety of marine life, including colorful fish and coral reefs.

In addition to natural features, the Costa Smeralda offers a variety of cultural experiences. Porto Cervo, noted for its luxury yachts and high-end shopping, is one popular location. Visitors can meander around the streets, enjoy the gorgeous architecture, and sample some of the local food at one of the many restaurants.

Another cultural feature is the Arzachena Museum, which depicts the region's history and culture. The museum has displays on ancient civilizations, traditional crafts, and Sardinia's natural environment.

Finally, no trip to the Costa Smeralda would be complete without eating some of the local cuisine. The area is well-known for its fresh seafood, which includes lobster, sea bass, and octopus. Visitors can also sample typical Sardinian meals such as porceddu (roasted pig), culurgiones (a sort of ravioli), and pane carasau (a thin, crispy bread).

IV. Things to Do

Beaches

If you're visiting Sardinia for the first time and searching for a beach escape, here's all you need to know about the island's beaches.

Sardinia's beaches are diverse and appeal to all tastes, from isolated bays to busy resorts. The Costa Smeralda, or northeast portion of the island, is home to some of the most famous beaches. The Costa Smeralda is well-known for its clean waters, fine white sand, and opulent resorts. Capriccioli, Porto Cervo, and Liscia Ruja are the most popular beaches on the Costa Smeralda.

The southwest part of Sardinia, known as the Costa del Sud, is another renowned beach area. This region is well-known for its lengthy expanses of sandy beach, turquoise waters, and rocky coves. Chia, Tuerredda, and Porto Pino have some of the most stunning beaches on the Costa del Sud.

If you want a less crowded, less touristic beach experience, come to Sardinia's west coast. The west coast is less urbanized and has a more rocky scenery than the east shore. Is Arutas, San Giovanni di Sinis, and Bosa Marina are among the most stunning beaches on the west coast.

Head to the Maddalena Archipelago for a really unique beach experience. The Maddalena Archipelago is a series of islands off Sardinia's northeast coast. The archipelago is a protected national park with some of Sardinia's most picturesque beaches. Cala Corsara, Spalmatore, and

Cala Granara are the most well-known beaches in the Maddalena Archipelago.

Tourists can enjoy a range of activities on Sardinia's beaches. Snorkeling and scuba diving are popular hobbies in Sardinia, and many beaches provide equipment rentals as well as guided tours. Try windsurfing, kiteboarding, or sailing for a more active beach experience.

Many of Sardinia's beaches have beach bars, restaurants, and stores as amenities. Some of the more popular beaches hire out loungers and umbrellas. It's worth mentioning that some of the more remote beaches may not have any amenities, so carry your own.

Finally, it's critical to understand Sardinia's beach restrictions. Some beaches are protected zones, and activities such as fishing, mooring boats, and bringing dogs may be prohibited. Before going to the beach, always verify the local restrictions.

Amazing Story of a Couple

Deborah and Peter were first-time visitors to Sardinia and were looking forward to exploring the island's beaches. They'd heard about the stunning shoreline and wanted to see it for themselves. They chose to visit the Costa Smeralda and the island's southwest section.

Capriccioli beach in the Costa Smeralda was their first stop. The crystal-clear waters and lovely white beach astounded them. They rented lounge chairs and umbrellas and spent the day on the beach relaxing. They also went snorkeling and were astounded by the underwater life they observed.

They then went to Chia beach in the southwest region. The blue waves and lengthy expanse of sandy beach were magnificent. They tried windsurfing and had a great time riding the waves. They also ate fish at one of the beachfront eateries.

Deborah and Peter went on a trip to the Maddalena Archipelago and were blown away by the beautiful beaches. They went on a boat cruise and saw various islands, including Spalmatore Beach. The rugged landscape and crystal-clear waterways were remarkable.

Deborah and Peter were impressed by the amenities available at the beaches during their stay. They appreciated the beach bars, restaurants, and stores, and thought the rental equipment was excellent.

Deborah and Peter had a fantastic day touring Sardinia's beaches. They were impressed by the variety of beaches and activities available. They highly recommend Sardinia as a beach destination.

Hiking and Nature

The island is brimming with great hiking routes that showcase the region's natural splendor. Sardinia has it all, from towering mountains to breathtaking beach views. In this article, we'll look at the best hiking routes in Sardinia and discover the natural beauties that await.

The Selvaggio Blu, a hard 6-day trip through some of Sardinia's most remote and magnificent scenery, is one of the island's most popular hiking trails. The trail is a 50-kilometer route that follows the island's eastern shore, providing hikers with breathtaking vistas of the Mediterranean's turquoise waters. The trail is known for its natural beauty, with breathtaking views of cliffs, gorges, and secret beaches. The trail, however, is not for the faint of heart, since it requires a high level of fitness and a solid sense of location.

The Gola di Gorropu trek is ideal for people searching for a shorter, more doable hike. The trail leads hikers into a narrow ravine with towering rock formations on either side. The valley is one of Europe's deepest, and the walk provides stunning views of the canyon walls and crystal-clear streams below. The walk is quite straightforward, making it suitable for hikers of all skill levels.

The Tiscali Nuragic Village Trail is yet another popular hiking trail in Sardinia. The trail leads hikers through the heart of the island, providing breathtaking views of the mountains and valleys. The old Nuragic town of Tiscali, which is housed inside a big natural cave, is the trail's highlight. The village dates back to the Bronze Age and provides an intriguing peek into Sardinia's rich cultural heritage.

The Cala Goloritze Trail is a fantastic option for people seeking for a beach hike. The walk leads hikers along the magnificent coastline of the Gulf of Orosei, providing breathtaking views of the crystal-clear waters and craggy cliffs. The trail's centerpiece is the gorgeous Cala Goloritze beach, which is regarded as one of the most beautiful in the world. The beach is only accessible by foot or boat, making it a private and peaceful hideaway.

Sardinia also has various natural parks with excellent hiking options. The Gennargentu National Park, which spans over 700 square kilometers of rugged terrain, is one of the most popular. The park contains various hiking paths that lead hikers through some of the most beautiful scenery on the island, including deep canyons, lush woods, and high peaks. The park is also home to a variety of species, including wild boars, eagles, and Sardinian deer.

Finally, Sardinia's natural beauty extends to its beaches and shoreline. The island has some of the most beautiful beaches in the world, with crystal-clear waters and silky white sand. Because many of the beaches are only accessible by foot or boat, they are ideal for hiking. The coastline also has various hiking routes that provide breathtaking views of the sea and the rough rocks.

Finally, Sardinia is a hiker's heaven, with a vast selection of paths showcasing the island's natural beauties. Sardinia has something for everyone, from rough mountain peaks to magnificent seaside views. Hikers will find several attractions on the island, including natural parks, ancient settlements, and isolated beaches. Whether you're a seasoned hiker or a newbie, Sardinia is the ideal spot for your next hiking excursion.

Food and Wine

Sardinia is an Italian island in the Mediterranean Sea. Its cuisine is distinguished by the use of fresh and local products, which are frequently prepared utilizing traditional cooking methods. The island is also known for its wine production, which dates back to ancient times. In this post, we will look at Sardinia's unique culinary culture and wine traditions.

Sardinian Cuisine:

Sardinian cuisine is greatly impacted by the island's topography, history, and culture. Seafood is popular along the island's coast, but meat and cheese are more common inland. The most famous Sardinian cheese is Pecorino, which is manufactured from sheep's milk and is used in many local cuisines.

Sardinian gnocchi, also known as Malloreddus, is a popular dish in Sardinia. It's made with semolina flour and comes with a tomato and sausage sauce. Porceddu, a roasted suckling pig cooked over an open flame and seasoned with herbs and spices, is another favorite meal.

Other classic Sardinian foods include Fregula, a pasta dish prepared with toasted semolina, saffron, and clams, and Culurgiones, which are handmade pasta stuffed with potatoes and cheese.

Wine in Sardinia:

Sardinia is well-known for its wine production, which stretches back more than 3,000 years. The island's climate and soil make it excellent for wine production. The most well-known Sardinian wines are Vermentino, Cannonau, and Carignano.

Vermentino is a white wine with a fresh and fruity flavor. It is frequently served with seafood and is an excellent complement to the local cuisine.

Cannonau is a red wine created from the Grenache grape. It is a full-bodied wine with a high alcohol concentration that is frequently combined with meat meals.

Carignano is a red wine created from the Carignan grape. It is a full-bodied, rich wine that is often matured in wood barrels.

Winemaking in Sardinia is still quite traditional, with many winemakers producing their wines using ancient processes. Many vineyards are open to the public for tours and tastings, which is a terrific way to learn about the local wine culture.

Nightlife and Entertainment

Sardinia has something for everyone, whether you want a relaxing night out or a raucous party.

Porto Cervo, located on the island's northern coast, is one of the most popular nightlife spots in Sardinia. This expensive vacation town is popular among the international jet set, with several pubs, clubs, and restaurants. You may dance the night away at elite nightclubs like Billionaire Club, where you might spy a celebrity or two, or enjoy a more laid-back vibe at the elegant Phi Beach Club.

Cagliari, the island's capital, is also a popular nightlife destination in Sardinia. The city has a bustling environment and a range of entertainment alternatives, including bars, clubs, and theaters. La Mela di Newton, a bustling discotheque where you can dance to the newest hits and enjoy a terrific environment, is a popular venue.

If you're seeking for something more unusual, the city of Alghero has a variety of entertainment possibilities. The old town is filled of small taverns and cafes ideal for a drink or two with friends. Alternatively, you might visit the Teatro Civico, a lovely theater that holds a variety of cultural events and plays throughout the year.

Sardinia also has enough to offer those seeking a more casual evening experience. Many towns and villages on the island hold traditional festivals and celebrations throughout the year, which are a terrific chance to learn about local culture and traditions. During the annual Autunno in Barbagia festival, for example, you can see traditional Sardinian folk music and dancing in the town of Orgosolo.

Aside from nightlife, Sardinia has a variety of daytime activities for travelers. The island's beautiful beaches are popular for sunbathing and swimming, while the crystal-clear seas are ideal for snorkeling and scuba diving. You can also visit the island's various historic and cultural landmarks, like as the ancient ruins of the Nuragic civilization or the spectacular Cattedrale di Santa Maria in Sassari.

Overall, Sardinia has a varied selection of nightlife and entertainment opportunities for travellers. Whether you're looking for a crazy night out or a more tranquil one, there's plenty to do on this magnificent island in the center of the Mediterranean. Sardinia is the ideal location for anyone looking for an exceptional holiday experience, thanks to its distinct culture, outstanding natural beauty, and dynamic environment.

Events and Festivals

Throughout the year, the island hosts a range of events and festivals that allow visitors to immerse themselves in Sardinia's distinct culture and traditions. If you're a first-time visitor to the island, here are some of the top events and festivals you shouldn't miss.

The Sagra del Redentore, held in Nuoro in August, is one of the most popular festivals in Sardinia. This festival celebrates the harvest season and includes traditional costumes, music, and dance. The festival's climax is a procession of the Madonna del Redentore, a statue of the Virgin Mary carried through the streets of Nuoro by locals.

Another must-see event in Sardinia is the Cavalcata Sarda, which takes place in Sassari in May. This festival honors the island's equestrian heritage with a parade of horses and riders costumed in traditional Sardinian attire. During the festival, attendees can also enjoy traditional Sardinian food and music.

The Time in Jazz festival in Berchidda is a must-see for jazz fans. This annual jazz festival, held in August, featuring performances by some of the world's best jazz musicians. The event also includes workshops and masterclasses for aspiring musicians.

If you're interested in history, the Sant'Efisio festival in Cagliari is a must-see. This festival commemorates Cagliari's patron saint and dates back to the 17th century. The centerpiece of the celebration is a parade of the saint's statue through the streets of the city, attended by locals dressed in traditional costumes.

The Autunno in Barbagia festival is a must-see for culinary lovers. This festival, held in the Sardinian region of Barbagia in September and October, showcases typical Sardinian food and wine. Visitors can try a range of meals, including suckling pig, roasted lamb, and local cheeses.

Other prominent events and festivals in Sardinia include the Festa di San Giovanni in Sassari, the Festa di San Simplicio in Olbia, and the Sagra della Vela in Santa Teresa Gallura. These events allow tourists to immerse themselves in the distinctive culture and customs of Sardinia.

To summarize, Sardinia is a vibrant and diversified island with a rich cultural legacy. Whether you're like music, food, history, or equestrian customs, Sardinia has an event or festival for you. Don't miss out on these unique cultural events and festivals if you're a first-time visitor to the island.

V. Practical Information

Healthy Living

Sardinia is noted for its healthy lifestyle and its inhabitants' lifespan. If you are a first-time visitor to Sardinia, there are various things you can do to embrace a healthy lifestyle throughout your stay.

Diet is one of the most important components of living a healthy lifestyle, and Sardinia has a rich culinary culture that promotes health and longevity. Sardinian cuisine is based on a Mediterranean diet that emphasizes fruits, vegetables, whole grains, legumes, nuts, and seeds. The menu also contains fish and seafood, lean meats, and dairy items, all of which are consumed in moderation. Olive oil, which is high in healthful fats and antioxidants, is a staple of Sardinian cuisine. The island's cuisine also includes a variety of herbs and spices, which provide flavor and nutrition to dishes.

Pane carasau, a thin, crisp bread produced from durum wheat flour, is one of Sardinian cuisine's most recognizable dishes. Pane carasau is high in fiber and is frequently served with olive oil and tomato sauce. Another popular tourist food in Sardinia is culurgiones, a type of ravioli stuffed with potato, mint, and cheese. Culurgiones are often served with a tomato sauce and shredded pecorino cheese. Seafood fans will adore the Sardinian fregola con arselle, a typical pasta meal cooked with clams, tomato sauce, and fresh herbs.

In addition to a healthy diet, Sardinia provides numerous chances for physical activity. The stunning shoreline of the island is ideal for swimming, snorkeling, and diving. The island's rugged interior provides options for trekking, cycling, and rock climbing. Sardinia also contains various nature reserves that are home to a diverse range of flora and fauna. The island's biodiversity includes wild boars, deer, eagles, and various uncommon bird species.

Sardinia's pleasant temperature and abundance of sunshine also make it a great destination for outdoor activities. The island includes various beaches that are ideal for sunbathing and swimming. Visitors can also participate in water sports such as windsurfing, kiteboarding, and sailing. Sardinia's mild winters allow for year-round outdoor sports, and the island boasts several ski resorts that offer skiing and snowboarding during the winter months.

Sardinia provides a relaxing and stress-free lifestyle in addition to a nutritious diet and physical activity.

The people of the island are noted for their kindness and hospitality, and they place a high emphasis on family, community, and tradition. Sardinia hosts a number of festivals and cultural events throughout the year, allowing visitors to immerse themselves in the island's rich cultural legacy. Visitors can also explore the island's ancient ruins, churches, and museums, which display the island's history and art.

How to Stay Safe

While Sardinia is typically a safe place to visit, there are several precautions that travellers can take to protect their safety while on the island. In this piece, we'll go over some safety tips for Sardinia.

Be aware of your surroundings

It is critical to be alert of your surroundings in this, as in any tourist location. Keep an eye out for any unusual behavior and avoid going alone at night, especially in less populated areas. Keep an eye on your belongings and be wary of pickpockets if you're in a crowded area.

Be careful when driving

If you plan to rent a car while in Sardinia, drive carefully. The roads can be small and twisty, and some drivers might be irresponsible. Wear your seatbelt at all times and avoid driving under the influence of drugs or alcohol.

Take sun protection measures.

Sardinia may get very hot in the summer, therefore sun protection is essential. Wear sunscreen with a high SPF, as well as a hat and sunglasses to protect your face and eyes. Drink plenty of water to keep hydrated.

Swim with caution.

Sardinia is famous for its stunning beaches and crystal-clear waters, however swimming should be done with caution. Always swim in approved locations and be mindful of any warning signs or flags. Never swim alone, and be wary of rip currents.

Respect the local culture.

Sardinia has a rich cultural legacy, and it is crucial to respect the local culture while visiting the island. When visiting churches or other religious locations, dress appropriately and avoid snapping photos of locals without their consent. If you're unclear about local customs or etiquette, seek assistance from a local.

Keep your valuables safe

Keep valuables such as passports, money, and devices in a secure location. When traveling, use a hotel safe or a locked bag, and avoid carrying big sums of cash. Be wary of anyone who tries to distract you or divert your attention away from your belongings.

Be prepared for emergencies

While Sardinia is generally a safe destination to visit, it is vital to be prepared for emergencies. Make a plan in case of an emergency, such as a natural disaster or a medical issue. Carry a copy of your passport and other necessary paperwork, and be sure you have travel insurance that covers medical emergencies.

Money and Budgeting

If you're visiting Sardinia for the first time, it's crucial to grasp the local currency and budgeting alternatives. Sardinia is a picturesque island in the Mediterranean Sea noted for its spectacular beaches, mountainous mountains, and distinct culture. However, as with any tourist destination, managing your finances while on vacation is critical to ensuring a smooth and pleasurable trip. Here's a guide about money and budgeting in Sardinia for first-time visitors.

Sardinia's currency is:

The Euro (EUR) is Sardinia's official currency. The euro is widely accepted throughout the European Union and is easily accessible through banks and exchange offices. It's always a good idea to exchange your currency before arriving in Sardinia, as exchange rates can vary based on your location. If you're in a hurry, you can also exchange money at the airport or local banks. Credit and debit cards are frequently accepted in Sardinia, particularly in tourist destinations. However, it is always a good idea to keep some cash on hand for modest expenditures and emergencies.

Cost of living in Sardinia:

The cost of living in Sardinia is often greater than in the rest of Italy, especially during the peak tourist season. However, with proper preparation and budgeting, it is feasible to enjoy the island's offers without breaking the bank. The cost of meals, lodging, and transportation will vary according to your location and the time of year you visit. Staying at a premium resort on Costa Smeralda, the island's most exclusive area, for example, will be significantly more expensive than a budget-friendly lodging in a little village. Similarly, dining in a fine dining restaurant in the city center will be more expensive than eating at a small pizzeria.

Budgeting for Sardinia:

Here are some budgetary recommendations to help you plan your trip to Sardinia:

Plan ahead: Sardinia's busiest tourist season runs from June to September, so if feasible, plan your trip outside of these months. Prices are often lower during the off-season, and you'll avoid the crowds.

Choose your lodging wisely: The sort of lodging you select will have a big impact on your budget. Consider staying in a local hamlet or town rather than a tourist hub, and explore for budget-friendly choices such as hostels, campsites, and vacation rentals.

Explore local markets: Sardinia is famed for its wonderful food, and exploring local markets is a great way to enjoy the island's gastronomic delights. Stock up on fresh produce, cheese, and cured meats for a low-cost picnic or supper.

Use public transportation: Sardinia has an extensive bus network that connects most major villages and cities. Taking public transit is a cost-effective way to get around the island, especially if you're traveling alone or in a small group.

Take advantage of free activities: One of Sardinia's main draws is its natural beauty, and there are numerous free things to enjoy. Hiking, cycling, and visiting beaches are just a few examples of free activities.

Fast internet Connection in Sardinia

If you are a first-time visitor to Sardinia, you may be curious about the island's internet connectivity. Sardinia, thankfully, has a well-developed internet infrastructure with a number of options for fast internet connections.

Fiber-optic internet is one of the most popular choices for fast internet in Sardinia. Fiber-optic internet transmits data via light, resulting in substantially quicker rates than typical copper cable internet. TIM, Vodafone, and WindTre are just a few of the companies in Sardinia that provide fiber-optic internet access. These providers provide plans with varied speeds and data limitations, so you should compare them to choose the one that best meets your needs.

Mobile internet is yet another choice for fast internet in Sardinia. Many cell operators on the island provide 4G and 5G services, which can be a useful choice for travellers that require on-the-go internet connection. Because mobile internet plans often provide a set amount of data each month, it's critical to keep track of your consumption to avoid unexpected penalties. In Sardinia, popular mobile service providers include TIM, Vodafone, WindTre, and Iliad.

You may have access to Wi-Fi while staying in a hotel or vacation rental in Sardinia. Most hotels and vacation rentals provide Wi-Fi to their visitors, and some may charge a fee for high-speed Wi-Fi. When booking your accommodations, check to see if Wi-Fi is included, as well as the speed and data allowance.

There are also internet cafes and public Wi-Fi stations around Sardinia. If you need to check your email or do some light browsing while you're out and about, these can be helpful solutions. However, when utilizing public Wi-Fi, you should exercise caution because it is less secure than a private connection.

Overall, whether you are looking for a fiber-optic connection, mobile internet, Wi-Fi, or a public hotspot, Sardinia has a number of options for fast internet connectivity. When selecting an internet plan, keep in mind your data requirements and consumption habits, as well as any additional fees or charges that may apply. You can stay connected and enjoy all that Sardinia has to offer with a little research and effort.

Transportation

If you plan to visit this lovely island, understanding how to move around is essential for a smooth and pleasurable vacation.

Buses, railways, taxis, and vehicle rentals are the main modes of transportation on the island. Here is a complete guide on getting about Sardinia:

By Bus: Buses are a popular and inexpensive means of transportation in Sardinia, with services covering the island's major towns and cities. There are several types of buses to meet a variety of demands and budgets. The ARST is Sardinia's principal bus company, offering both urban and intercity routes. If you intend to travel great distances, it is best to buy your tickets in advance. The buses are typically pleasant and air-conditioned, with some having complimentary Wi-Fi.

By Train: Sardinia has a small rail network, with services serving only a few sections of the island. Trenitalia operates the trains, and the main lines run from Cagliari to Sassari, Cagliari to Olbia, and Sassari to Porto Torres. Train travel is slower than other kinds of transportation, but it is an excellent alternative if you want to enjoy the lovely landscape along the way. The trains are frequently on time, and the tickets are reasonable.

Taxis are commonly available in Sardinia and are a good option for short excursions or if you choose not to drive. Taxis in Sardinia are typically white with a 'TAXI' sign on top. They can be hailed on the street or booked through a taxi company. Fares are normally metered, however it's best to clarify the amount before the ride to avoid any surprises.

Car Rental: If you want to explore Sardinia at your own pace, renting a car is the ideal alternative. Sardinia has a well-developed road network, and driving is reasonably simple. You can rent a car at the airport or in one of the major cities. It is best to book ahead of time, especially during high season. The rental fees vary based on the type of automobile and the rental business, but they are generally reasonable.

Driving in Sardinia: Driving in Sardinia is reasonably simple, thanks to a well-developed road network that spans the entire island. The traffic signs are in Italian, but the most of them are simple to comprehend. The speed limit in cities is normally 50 km/h, whereas on highways it is 130 km/h. It is important to note that roads can be small, especially in the countryside, and certain routes may have steep inclines, therefore it is best to rent a car with a powerful engine. Also, be wary of stray animals that may appear on the roads, especially at night.

Language and Communication

Sardinia has a primordial past and has been impacted by different civilizations throughout the years, notably the Phoenicians, Romans, and Spanish. As a result, the island has a distinct culture and language that is distinct from the rest of Italy.

Language and communication in Sardinia can be difficult for travelers, especially those who do not speak Italian. Sardinian, a Romance language, is also widely spoken on the island. Sardinian is, in reality, the region's second official language, and it is protected by regional legislation.

Sardinian is a very old language that is thought to be one of Europe's oldest Romance languages. It is a language that has been spoken on the island for thousands of years and has evolved into several dialects over time. Today, the island is home to various dialects of Sardinian, each with its own distinct characteristics.

Tourists visiting Sardinia should be aware that most residents speak both Italian and Sardinian, and they frequently switch between the two depending on the situation. Sardinian is the major language spoken in rural areas, whereas Italian is more widely spoken in metropolitan areas. However, most locals are fluent in both languages and are willing to switch between them to make communication easier for tourists.

While Sardinian may appear to be a tough language to learn, travellers can nevertheless make an effort to learn some fundamental phrases to make their vacation more pleasurable. Some important phrases to know include "bona sèra" (good evening), "gràtzias" (thank you), and "de sa ndie" (you're welcome). Learning some basic Sardinian phrases can also be a terrific approach to show respect for the local culture and connect with the locals.

Nonverbal signs and gestures can impact communication in Sardinia in addition to words. Locals, for example, are known for being quite expressive with their hands when they speak, and they frequently utilize gestures to underline their argument. Tourists should also be aware that eye contact is very essential in Sardinian culture, and not making eye contact might be interpreted as rudeness.

When speaking with natives in Sardinia, keep in mind that the culture is highly accepting and friendly. Sardinians are recognized for their generosity and joy of sharing their culture with others. Tourists that take the time to learn a few basic words and make an effort to engage with the locals will have a far more enjoyable and authentic experience.

Grand Finale

To summarize, Sardinia is a really unique place that provides a varied range of experiences that are likely to leave a lasting effect on anybody who visits. This magnificent island has something for everyone to enjoy, from its stunning beaches and rugged coasts to its charming towns and old ruins.

But it's not simply the natural beauty of Sardinia that distinguishes it; it's also the warmth and hospitality of its people, the rich history and culture that can be felt in every corner, and the exquisite food that will tempt your taste buds.

So, if you're seeking for a destination that will provide you with a memorable experience, Sardinia should be at the top of your list. Sardinia has it all, whether you're a history buff, a beach bum, a foodie, or simply searching for an adventure. Don't pass up the opportunity to discover this hidden treasure for yourself - book your trip to Sardinia today and experience everything this beautiful island has to offer!

Printed in Great Britain
by Amazon

23262751R00096